Interrupted

Jess Strickland

Copyright © Jess Strickland 2016

Published by Living Hope

Please visit www.thisishope.com
for more information.

*There Is One Who Is Faithful
To Interrupt Your Life*

INTERRUPTED

Jess Strickland

 Living Hope
Aloha, OR

CONTENTS

CHAPTER 1 Prelude	*1*
CHAPTER 2 The Clock Read Eight	*5*
CHAPTER 3 Watts's World	*8*
CHAPTER 4 Between First and Second	*13*
CHAPTER 5 The Journey	*24*
CHAPTER 6 The World	*29*
CHAPTER 7 Counterclockwise Screws	*32*
CHAPTER 8 Weary	*35*

CHAPTER 9   *42*
The Voice

CHAPTER 10   *46*
Sustained

CHAPTER 11   *53*
Whispers and Fog

CHAPTER 12   *57*
A Sober Note

CHAPTER 13   *63*
Epilogue

*For those who go through stuff and find their
confidence a touch shaky,*

but especially for
my wife Brenda
*whose prayers Jesus favored
on behalf of my life.*

CHAPTER 1

Prelude

They were finishing their pre-surgery routines – they being the incredible nurse force of Good Samaritan, and I do mean incredible. The anesthesiologist pulled back the curtain and introduced himself. As he rehearsed the procedure, I remember thinking, "I should come out from under anesthesia around 1:30pm—if later, that would mean there was trouble."

A few minutes later, they began pushing my gurney, and then it was lights out.

About forty days before my surgery, I was led by Jesus to write a declaration built off of John 16.

*"I am not the sum total of what I think I am,
Nor what others think me to be.
I am not the calculated equivalence of my good
    deeds,
Nor am I the subtracted residue of my evil ones.*

*I am finite, with no point of honest appraisal,
Apart from He who transcends me.
I am, thus, what He says, and when I say He,
I mean the capital "H" He – Jesus.*

*Jesus defines me completely,
His word is absolute, the abiding truth.
Jesus says, "Peace I leave you,
My peace I give you."*

*This life gives fear, terror, panic.
Jesus gives peace, not the end of fear,
But the end of the cause of fear.*

*Jesus says, "I am going away."
Jesus says, "I will come to you."*

The cause of fear, terror and panic burned and melted,
In one assurance – "I will come to you."

I am the one who Jesus comes to, not because
I have earned Him, receive Him or obligate Him.

I am the one who Jesus comes to,
because God is good to His word.

I am the one Jesus comes to,
in favor, in fellowship and with blessing.

I was uncomfortable with this declaration, uncomfortable with how it turned out. Usually, when I engage in such a prayerful and maybe even prophetic style of writing, it just doesn't have so many "I's" involved. Sitting at my desk, reading over this declaration and being tempted to re-craft it, to rid it of the uncomely "I's," I felt persuaded against the notion. And I let it stand as written.

If you were to look in my journal, you would notice the phrase "I will come to you" is highlighted in red. There it was, there was my assurance – Jesus would come to me, right there in Scripture. And I was reiterated afresh, in my spirit, to write it down and embrace it; Jesus would come to me.

I remember in the ICU, squinting out through my eyes, off to the left, just above my head. And there I saw a clock. It was just after 8pm.

CHAPTER 2

THE CLOCK
READ EIGHT

I AM TOLD I HAD A TOUGH TIME WAKING UP. The doctors informed my wife of this (family members are told when patients who do not wake on time). Plenty of things could have gone wrong, and my wife's list included the possibility they might need to reopen me, to stop potential bleeding. I was still asleep, and my worst concerns were taking place – my wife was having to receive such news, concerning my condition, when I wasn't there to be with her. I had hoped to be out of the operating room, and awake, after an average interval. It was not to be. My wife had to sweat out the maybes for a few hours, until I began to emerge from surgery slumber.

I remember seeing the clock, I remember hating the tube down my throat. I remember male voices discussing whether or not they should take it out, I remember yelling in my mind, "For the love of God take it out!" I don't remember it being taken out. Later, I do remember some people being in the room, visiting me. Others were there whom I don't remember, so I won't list any names. I remember them telling my wife she could go home. I remember it was well after eight, and I remember being at peace.

Here is what I do remember in those early minutes of being awake in ICU. "I will come to you." I remember those words, I remember in my fuzzy mind, thinking, "I don't know what all has happened, but I do know this, You, Jesus, have come to me at the other side of this thing just like you promised. I went to sleep that first night, yes, under the fog of pain relievers, but also very aware that He had come to me and had been with me in a special way through surgery. I had no idea if there were complications or problems or other things I should know about, I just knew He had come to me, and his coming to me was a "Joy" breaking into my world.

CHAPTER 3

Watts's World

It's been a few days, but I have come to wonder about "Joy to the World" and the phrase "for God so loved the world." It leaves me asking, "What world?" No doubt, post-surgery joy had met me on the other side. Jesus came to me as He promised. But the question lingers in my heart, "What world is God so determined to love and bring His joy into?"

He certainly brought it into my surgery world, but, even as I edit this chapter, radicals have pillaged Paris with a carnage unbelievable to a sensible person.

There are close, deeply close friends, and people my wife and I deeply love, battling disease beyond my own ability to fathom.

We have such heroic people all around us, but my heart still cries out for those in pain. Where's the joy in their world?

I'm a pastor, I've not endeavored to be "homogenously" surrounded by only the healthy and affluent, but also to be near those seeking Jesus. So we are a mixed bag of folks. My point is – with all the joy and rejoicing, we also see a great deal of pain. There are tears flowing, voices quivering, hearts racing, and the question remains. Where is the joy in their world?

In wanting to make the clearest sense of a little Christmas Hymn (one of my favorites, "Joy to the World"), I have sought to understand what world joy has joy come to. And, further keeping stride with John 3:16, what world does God so love?

The lyrics of "Joy to the World" were written by Isaac Watts, who was a prolific hymn writer, composing some 750 songs. A touch of background on Watts might prove helpful when considering the hymn he wrote. At Watts's birth, his father was imprisoned as a nonconformist, meaning he would not embrace the spiritually dead state Church of England. Watts, the first born of nine children, was literally nursed on the jailhouse steps.

Watts grew up a prodigy, having learned Latin by four, Greek by nine, French by eleven, and Hebrew by thirteen. Suitors offered to pay for his education at Oxford or Cambridge, which would have assured him high position in the Anglican Church. Instead, at sixteen, he went to London and studied at a nonconformist independent academy, following in the steps of his father's more Biblical faith, and setting his destiny to be a nonconformist to the church of England.

As a child, Watts had a gift for rhyming, which agitated his father and for which Watts was whipped. From his father's whippings came this rhyme, "O father, do some pity take//And I will no more verses make."

After Watts left the academy, he returned home, at age twenty, for two years attending his father's church. He began to complain to his father about how the church was singing the psalms – without fervency. To Watts, their singing seemed like the singing of those who didn't really believe. Watts's father, tiring of his son's complaining, told him to do something about it. Watts did. He began that week writing hymns, and those two years, while staying in his father's home, he wrote some incredible hymns. While there were many who criticized Watts's hymns, saying that the singing of Psalms was more spiritual, Watts's hymns prevailed in the face of oppression. And eventually Isaac Watts became the father of modern hymns.

Watts eventually became the assistant pastor, and then the pastor, of Mark Lane's Independent Congregation in London, but due to sickness he soon resigned. He contracted a violent fever from which he never fully recovered. It was during this season of his life that he was received into the home of Sir Thomas Abney, who provided for Watts's care for the next thirty-six years.

Watts did ask a woman, Elizabeth Singer, to marry him. But Watts was a sickly man, his skin had a yellowish hue, his frame was frail, his stature only five foot, and his head disproportionate to his body. The woman who had fallen in love with his heart thus rejected his offer. After Singer met Watts, she stated, "though she loved the jewel, she could not admire the casket [case] which contained it." Watts never married.

This is the man who penned the words to the Christmas Hymn, "Joy to the World." Yet I must ask, what joy ever entered Watts's world?

CHAPTER 4

BETWEEN FIRST AND SECOND

ODDLY, THE HYMN WATTS PENNED WAS NOT written for Christmas, but to celebrate the second coming of Christ. "Joy to the World" was taken from Psalm 98, a psalm clearly celebrating Christ's second coming to earth.

So, before we can fully understand the hymn, "Joy to the World," take just a moment to see the words with which Watts was feeding his spirit before he wrote what we now enjoy as a Christmas carol.

I have provided Psalms 98:4-9 (from "The Message" translation) so that we might grasp the excitement by which Watts was stirred.

4 *Shout your praises to GOD, everybody!*
  Let loose and sing! Strike up the band!
5 *Round up an orchestra to play for GOD,*
  Add on a hundred-voice choir.
6 *Feature trumpets and big trombones,*
  Fill the air with praises to King GOD.
7 *Let the sea and its fish give a round of applause,*
  With everything living on earth joining in.
8 *Let ocean breakers call out, "Encore!"*
  And mountains harmonize the finale—
9 *A tribute to GOD when he comes,*
  When he comes to set the earth right.
  He'll straighten out the whole world,
  He'll put the world right, and everyone in it.

This Psalm is a "Thanksgiving psalm," and while we do not know, for certain, the identity of the author, many believe that Psalms 96 to 100 were written when David and Israel brought the Ark of the Covenant from the home of Obed-Edom to Jerusalem.

This is one of the Psalms likely written by David, or for David, to give thanks and great praise to God for returning His presence to the nation of Israel, as symbolized in the treasured Ark being brought to Jerusalem. David rejoiced because Yahweh was coming back into Israel's world.

Isaac Watts would have known all this history, and more. He would have considered the Messianic prophecy within the Psalm, and would have considered God in Christ setting the earth right when he read these words of the Psalm – "He'll straighten out the whole world."

Notice the words "joy to the world" are not in Psalm 98. Isaac Watts transliterates, or translates, the action of 'joy to the world' to mean that when Christ comes, He will straighten the world all out.

It's a small point, but one that must be made; the Psalmist calls for everyone in Israel to pick up an instrument and praise Yahweh with great joy for what He will do, not what He has done.

Yes, God coming to the world, in this Psalm, was believed to be His second coming because only in His second coming will He ultimately straighten the whole world out.

I may as well let you know that I do have an argument with such a literal approach to the first and second coming of Jesus. Should we so systematically divide the first and second coming, when in the Old Testament Yahweh describes the first and second coming of Jesus so clumsily. What I mean by 'clumsy' is this: when the Old Testament prophets would prophesy about the Messiah's coming, they would seem to not comprehend what was the work of His first coming, and what would He subsequently do at His second coming. And they would seem to mix both up in the same prophecy.

A great example of this is found in the words Jesus declared from Isaiah, as the course of his ministry (Isaiah 61:1-2 NLT).

The Spirit of the Sovereign LORD is upon me,
for the LORD has anointed me
to bring good news to the poor.
He has sent me to comfort the brokenhearted
and to proclaim that captives will be released
and prisoners will be freed.*
He has sent me to tell those who mourn
that the time of the LORD's favor has come,*
and with it, the day of God's anger
against their enemies.

The above words are from Isaiah, but when Jesus uses this passage as the declaration of how Yahweh will shape His ministry, Jesus leaves off the last line – "and with it, the day of God's anger against their enemies." Isaiah included the line as part of the Messiah's work when He came to earth, but Jesus omitted the last line because the last line was not his focus during his earthly ministry.

This is why scholars have observed that, after Christ was born, He did such and such during his first coming, and then these same scholars have tended to shove everything else off to be done at His second coming.

Yes, I do have difficulty with all of this. I'm not sure there is actually a second coming in the literal sense that someone has left and will now return. (Don't get angry yet, hang in there and keep reading, it might get good.)

Traditionally, one might think that Jesus came, Jesus left, and Jesus is coming back. The logic works like this – we know He left because we cannot see Him.

To me, it might be more accurately described like this – Jesus came, He's here, He's invisible, He will reappear from behind the clouds and it will seem to us like He came again.

I get it, I am splitting hairs. But the splitting is important on so many levels.

Jesus will not only come some day to set the world straight, Jesus has already come and is presently setting the world straight. He did not quit what He started. Jesus did not come only to say, "Hi," and then give us the, "this is how you are healed and saved while the whole world rots under its own torment, but I promise I'll be back when the whole world is a festering cesspool of death and get my revenge then."

I think what has been traditionally understood as the first and second coming of Jesus can be better characterized as one coming and two great appearances. (1 Timothy 6:14; 2 Timothy 4:1; Titus 2:13; Hebrews 9:28; 1 Peter 5:4; 1 John 2:28).

Joy to the world, Jesus came to start the process of straightening the world out, and He will one day reappear to finish what He started to do with us.

Between the two great appearings of Jesus, He appears through His Holy Spirit, within His body, or among His people.

What I am seeking to point out in this chapter is that Jesus was coming to Isaac Watts's world to straighten things out. Watts captured the essence of what God was doing, and, with his gift of theology and rhyme, he began penning a declaration.

Watts read Psalms 98, and "Joy to the World" fell out of the Scripture. It became a declaration, and has been sung the world over, especially at Christmas time.

He did exactly what Jesus did when Jesus read Psalm 61 and realized it was a promise His Father had left Him and that it would become the declarative statement of His life mission.

Watts was a man whose life did nothing but go down; down from a position in the church of England to a motley band of ridiculed nonconformists; down from health to sickness; down from being attractive to repulsive; down from holding position in that motley church to being a patron of a rich man's compassion; down from being loved by a woman to having his body be too hideous to fully be loved. Down, rejected, subject to unfulfilled dreams; and yet what carried such a man? His declarations in song.

Now capture the hymn Watts wrote:

Joy to the world, the Lord is come!
Let earth receive her King;
Let every heart prepare Him room,
And Heaven and nature sing,
And Heaven and nature sing,
And Heaven, and Heaven, and nature sing.

Joy to the earth, the Savior reigns!
Let men their songs employ;
While fields and floods, rocks, hills and plains
Repeat the sounding joy,
Repeat the sounding joy,
Repeat, repeat, the sounding joy.

No more let sins and sorrows grow,
Nor thorns infest the ground;
He comes to make His blessings flow
Far as the curse is found,
Far as the curse is found,
Far as, far as, the curse is found.

He rules the world with truth and grace,
And makes the nations prove
The glories of His righteousness,
And wonders of His love,
And wonders of His love,
And wonders, wonders, of His love.

Down, down, down seems Watts's life. But the penning of this declaration perches him in a different world – a world of joy, and a world of festive thanksgiving. The world Watts paints in the hymn is one where the presence of a Savior frustrates the growth of sin, and causes blessings to flow everywhere the curse is found. Watts seems to be saying, in this declaration that became a hymn: Jesus rules, not Watts's own fever, sickness, or his ill-figured body; not the rejection of a woman, not even the persecution which came from being a hymn writer. No, in Watts's spirit, it was Jesus who ruled.

For Watts, between the first and second appearings of Jesus, there seems to be a place of joy where Jesus yet lives. It is how Jesus lives in us, between the first and second appearings, which will determine so much regarding our ultimate destiny. I realize we can't see Him, but my posture is that Jesus is more present than we can imagine. I can't see radio waves, but I can listen to voices, even live voices because they exist. We can't see Jesus between His appearings, but we can hear Him, and what we hear and speak may be the most significant part of our future.

CHAPTER 5

THE JOURNEY

I BEGAN MY HEART JOURNEY LAST MARCH, when it came to my attention that there was a blockage, known as the widow maker, in the left descending artery. I immediately determined to follow four guiding principles of health and healing.

1. Give your body to God to heal naturally.
2. Give your body to God to heal supernaturally.
3. Give your body to God to heal medically.
4. Give your body to God to heal invasively.

When I'm sick, I need to eat right, sleep right, rest right, exercise right, and take vitamins. In

America, the eat right thing is not easy. If eighty percent of the time I am eating well (and by eating well I mean that eighty percent of what is on my plate is vegetables), I will be eating healthy.

Any drink this, take this, buy this notion of dieting, or weight loss, is foolish for me to even consider. I understand that this might appeal to those seeking a diet for building muscle, but I needed a practical, life-long agenda of health. I must make sure eighty percent of what I eat is vegetable, and I must do this eighty percent of the time, and I must harshly eliminate, from my diet, sugars, starches, bad oils, dairy products, and processed foods. Yes, that leaves me with about four meals a week where I get to eat lamb, or some wild game. What a treat.

My point is not that I trust what I eat ahead of God, my point is that I revere and obey God's obvious natural care for my body. I do this so that I can put myself in a place to enjoy His health.

Second, I do not forget the supernatural healing power of God. Throughout my entire journey,

Brenda and I have loaded our time with prayer. So many supernatural things have and are taking place. While I have had surgery to remedy my heart, there are still so many other miracles God wants to do, and is doing. More than ever I am a believer in the gift of healing that is empowered by Christ's Holy Spirit. More than ever do I believe those gifts should be released to the world.

Third, where and when natural healing through Jesus, or supernatural healing through Jesus, does not seem to be working, one must acknowledsge that it is time to drink or take the medicine. I tried everything I knew, everything I could, and yet there was no change. And so I went to medicine. To me, medicine means things that may not be food, or plant-based. You know those things advertised on TV, which spend more time explaining what could go wrong by ingesting the product than what could go right. I don't start with medicine ever; it is third on my list. Even now there are too many prescriptions I am taking, but I'm working with my doctor to see if I can stop taking them. I want to live under natural and supernatural healing as much as possible.

Fourth, in my case, the treatment had to be invasive; and it was the invasive means that God has used for my healing. I didn't start here. I had time, and so I went to my healing declaration – those four steps I just listed, crafted from Scripture, and, I believe, inspired by God.

There have been critics to my approach, those who have neutrally listened, doctors who have been unhappy with my decisions, some friends who've thought me foolish. A few just snickered, but in my heart I believe I took the God-honoring road, and stayed under His leadership and directive.

I have learned that listening to Jesus can only be done in a vacuum. There is always some voice or opinion seeking to suck you down, some dark hole of doubt. Always something to bump you off of Scripture and into the dark shadows of doubt and pessimism.

So what keeps you from those holes of doubt, what keeps you in the fresh air of "joy to the world"?

Right before surgery, Brenda got a hold of something we wrote some years back, a "victory decree." And she began reading it – reading it for the power it might exert over herself and over me. That little declaration so settled my mind and spirit.

I actually had a secret list of things I wanted to get done before surgery, in case something happened to me. I had been working through the list for some weeks, bearing down on the last few items. As my wife began to read that decree over me, I felt a conviction in my heart against finishing the list. It was like God was saying to me, "what more do I need to do to tell you I will see you on the other side of this?"

I really do need to understand – "I am not the sum total of what I think I am."

CHAPTER 6

The World

I am seeking to build a theme that I hope you are hearing. So many join Christianity with their eyes on the morals, but it is not the morals Christ is seeking for us to adopt. Jesus does not want to make my life more ethically adaptable. He is wanting to make my heart Jesus-like in shape. He is not wanting me to be good, for I can never be good enough. But He is wanting to reshape my heart to be Jesus in shape. So what would a Jesus-shape heart look like? It would be a heart filled with faith.

The world we live in, by nature, dissipates faith, corrupts faith, destroys faith. If we are left to our own devices, to figure out what is good in this world, we may manufacture some God-like morality, but we will not have our hearts shaped to look like Jesus, or our hearts shaped to faith. Jesus was sinless because He never once distrusted His Father, He never lost faith, He never lived out His own idea of Himself.

God wants to shape that same faith in us, and the world is contrary to that shape. It is antagonistic to faith, disapproves of faith, and refuses to comply with faith at any level.

The world wants us to pursue comfort now, and urges us to follow what feels the most pleasant. Faith wants us to be more like pilgrims searching for the home that is coming down from heaven in the person of Jesus.

The world urges us to replenish ourselves at all reasonable costs, while faith calls upon us to deny ourselves and follow Jesus.

The world's voice is loud and obnoxious. Faith is quiet and tender and confident.

The world's voice demands immediacy. Faith seeks for time, and reoccurring obedience to grow what is longed for.

The world's voice screams, "Unfair." Faith says, "Jesus is straightening the world out."

So how is this "joy to the world" thing supposed to work in a world so contrary to Jesus?

CHAPTER 7

Counterclockwise Screws

The whole 'follow Jesus' thing can be incredibly confusing. The world around me looks one way, and the words of Jesus speak to me an opposing view. The direction His word speaks into me makes me feel contrary to the world, and yet being contrary to the world is not necessarily comfortable either.

I remember, as a boy, my Dad had these screws that screwed into metal, in reverse, or in a counterclockwise motion. These screws always confused me. For some reason, I couldn't wrap my mind around the fact that I had to turn them left in order make them go forward, or in. I further wondered why such screws were necessary, thinking their invention a silent ploy to confuse me. I was then informed that the vibration of machinery made right hand tightening screws easier to loosen. In other words, something had to be designed differently so that it would hold against the vibrations.

I suspect the same is true of the world we live in. Things must be designed differently if our lives are going to withstand all those vibrating voices surrounding us.

I have discovered, after years of study, experience, observation and trial, that the world lies. Yes, the world seems right, seems plausible, seems patently correct, seems reasonable, seems too formidable to challenge. But the truth? The world is not right and it's not too great to challenge. I realize the world is held by the power of Satan (Matthew 4:8-9; Luke 4:5-6), but his greatest power is deception (Revelation 12:9).

Yet, despite the grand-sounding symphony of worldly wisdom, the world is a liar, and our first steps back to Christ (and our continued steps in following Christ) depend on our ability to hear those lies, and to renounce them as the lies they are.

Yes, in the middle of this Christmas season, I want to take a moment to pen some words of rebellion against "the world of lies." If I am going to genuinely follow Jesus, I must be able to see through all the bold-faced, outrageously intimidating, behind the back, mocking lies the world tells me in avalanche proportion; and to confront those lies not with the good behavior of a moralist, but with Christ, and with faith in Christ.

If the world's voice is going to be confronted, if joy is really come, then the truth of the joy of His coming must drown out the damnable lies of this world. The screw must be turned counter to the world so it will hold firmly and unmistakably in Jesus, while all this shaking and vibrating continues around us.

CHAPTER 8

WEARY

I NEED TO FILL IN A LITTLE HISTORY TO DO this next part of my story. During the final days of Judah, as the Jews were defeated, and were being taken as captives out of Jerusalem, to Babylon, they left under the power of a prophetic declaration. Jeremiah said it this way: "For thus says the LORD: When seventy years are completed for Babylon, I will visit you, and I will fulfill to you my promise and bring you back to this place. For I know the plans I have for you, declares the LORD, plans for welfare and not for evil, to give you a future and a hope" (Jeremiah 29:10-11 ESV).

Once in Babylon, Daniel began to remind the Jews of Jeremiah's declaration; and he reminded them that their seventy years were coming to an end. I imagine those Jews began to think about their return to Jerusalem, to rebuild the temple. I imagine them beginning to edit, re-script, condense, even polish, the Sacred Scriptures under the inspiration of the Holy Spirit. I then imagine them coming to the Psalms of Ascent (Psalms 120-134) and placing them in theBookof Psalms, not aware they were being placed within the Psalms for Jesus Himself to one day pray.

These Psalms of Ascent were sung, especially by those post-exile Jews who, three times a year, would return to Jerusalem to celebrate the three yearly feasts. In the feast of Passover, they would celebrate their remembrance of Yahweh's deliverance of them from Egypt. In the feast of Pentecost, they would celebrate their renewed commitment to Yahweh by bringing Him their first fruits, trusting His present blessing. In the feast of Tabernacles, they would celebrate in anticipation of the great blessings Yahweh would bring upon them in the future.

As they would depart their villages and cities, and then begin their ascent to the Temple in Jerusalem, they would sing these fifteen songs of Ascent. It was a way of reminding themselves of who Yahweh had made them to be, and where they were ultimately headed. As they climbed up toward Jerusalem, and sang these fifteen songs, they were allowing their hearts to renew their spiritual ascent to Yahweh.

There is no doubt Jesus sang these Psalms, and meditated on these Psalms, as His family was devoted to taking Jesus to worship in Jerusalem for each feast. These passages would have been formative in His view of how His Father brought change into the lives of people. This first Psalm, Psalm 120, renouncing the lies of the world, must have had an amazing impact on His spirit.

The Prayer

Psalms 120:1 "I took my troubles to the LORD; I cried out to him, and he answered my prayer."

The Concern

Psalms 120:2 "Rescue me, O LORD, from liars and from all deceitful people. 3 O deceptive tongue, what will God do to you? How will he increase your punishment? 4 You will be pierced with sharp arrows and burned with glowing coals.

The Weariness

Psalms 120:5 How I suffer in far-off Meshech. It pains me to live in distant Kedar. 6 I am tired of living among people who hate peace. 7 I search for peace; but when I speak of peace, they want war!

We see this Psalm divided into three separate sections.

First, the Psalmist announces what he has done; prayed with passion in his troubles and was answered.

Second, the Psalmist defines his troubles; his world is surrounded by liars and deceit, and he questions how long until God will increases His judgment against this world of lying and deceit, and destroy it.

Third, the Psalmist expresses weariness in waiting for the lying mouth of the world to be stopped and judged by God. Meshech was a place near Russia, while Kedar was a nomadic Bedouin tribe of hoodlums. In essence, the Psalmist is saying he is getting weary of living in a world filled with people whose souls are a long way from God, who stir up strife while pretending to want peace. From the Psalmist's perspective, the world is ever bent toward, and can never save itself from, being offended, becoming bitter, erupting into strife and ultimately killing, or murder.

What the Psalmist is saying here is that he is weary of the vibrating machinery of the world, which seeks to loosen his grip on trust.

Do you ever weary of the voices? Do you ever get tired of hearing what you can't do, or what will most likely happen (which is rarely good news)? Do you ever tire of being pulled in a direction you know is not good for your soul? Do you ever feel sorrow, knowing the voice you are leaning toward is not the voice of God?

The world is the atmosphere we live in, it is full of thoughts and notions almost always counter to God. Those far from God hardly notice the voice, and those who seek to believe, or even follow, Christ are greatly deceived by the voices.

These voices were present during the time of my surgery. Before surgery, these voices sought to create fear in me, minimizing the importance of Jesus and His word. These voices also sought to get me so relaxed with the process that Jesus would be marginalized; and I was encouraged to make the doctors the focus of my trust.

After surgery, the voices still rage, seeking to discourage me by reminding me of how long the process is taking. Then, on the other hand, they encourage me to exert myself before I am physically ready.

These voices are relentless; they will not shut up long enough for God to speak. And so the move toward the voice of God is always accomplished with a good deal of denial.

Hang in there. If you weary of the voices, there are two things yet to be done, as revealed in this Psalm. First, identify the voices, and then mercilessly obliterate them as a foreign terrorist to your soul.

Psalm 120 began with the conclusion. The Psalmist cried out to the Lord, and was heard, which meant he was rescued by piercing the voice of the world with sharp arrows and burning coals. He did not stop the voices everywhere, but he renounced them in his own heart, and stopped their influence upon his mind.

CHAPTER 9

THE VOICE

WHAT IS THE VOICE OF THE WORLD, WHICH is so counter to the voice of Christ? What voice needs to be discerned and then dethroned?

The voice of Advertisers: I can give you what you need!
The voice of Entertainers: I will make you happy!
The voice of Politicians: I can fix you!
The voice of Psychologists: I can re-shape you!
The voice of Pastors: I can heal you!
The voice of Preachers: I can inform you!
The voice of Moralists: I can make others owe you!

The voice of Cosmetologists: I can make young!
The voice of Designers: I can make you sexy!
The voice of Trainers: I can make feel powerful!
The voice of Economists: I can make you prosper!
The voice of Generals: I can keep you safe!
The voice of Doctors: I can almost always restore you!
The voice of Technologists: I can make your life easier!
The voice of Culture: you are stupid!
The voice of Self: I don't need God all the time!

I realize the list isn't complete. Each of the above voices makes more than one statement, and the list itself is not complete, but you get the idea. The world is constantly sounding its horn, promising to perform one thing when it cannot deliver what it promises. When I have been promised that something will make me happy, or well, or safe, or will be more convenient; and when that promise is left unfulfilled, I become disappointed, which can lead to bitterness, then to strife, and finally to killing.

The way of the world is simple. Its voice promises, but its voice cannot produce the results. Hurt leads to offense, which leads to bitterness, which leads to strife, which leads to some level of death. The world proceeds in the power of the evil one, and he has come to kill, steal and destroy (John 10:10). This is how he does it – the voice of the world lies, and we become hurt. This causes us to want to kill – relationships, or reputations, or anything else we can get our hands on. The machinery vibrates.

Do you see here what the Psalmist does in Psalm 120? Once again, he writes a declaration. He lets the voice of God move through his own soul until the breath of faith pours back out into the world of lies. When Jesus prayed this Psalm on His way to Jerusalem to worship with His family,

He was breathing God's Word into the world of lies, making room for joy in His soul.

Between Jesus's first appearing and his second appearing the Holy Spirit speaks Christ's word, through His followers. So with every breath we are making more space for joy in the world. When we boldly speak God's word, we are bringing His atmosphere to earth, and His atmosphere is giddy with joy.

CHAPTER 10

Sustained

It has been eighteen days since Jesus met me, according to promise, on the other side of surgery. Yes, medicine was great, the doctors more than incredible; all the many things which were done for me I am so grateful for, but at the end of the day I'm here because of Jesus.

I know we are really good at heart surgery, but they had my chest open. The number of other things that could've gone wrong is enormous. My wife, waiting all those hours for me to wake up, was given a mass of potentially bad outcomes. She was made to stand in my gap with the shroud of concern draped over her heart. In the end, there was nothing to report. If I weren't telling the story, few would know. Family members were sent home; reports went out that I was recovering well. But for those few hours there was an abundance of things that could yet go wrong. They were holding my eyelid open, yelling in my ear, doing things my wife told me later she wish she had not seen. So the question remains – why don't all the little things that could go wrong, or should go wrong, actually occur? For most people, the answer is Jesus, who upholds the universe and its details by the word of his power.

"The Son radiates God's own glory and expresses the very character of God, and he sustains everything by the mighty power of his command"(Hebrews 1:3 NLT). I guess when I look at this passage I'm surprised. I would've thought the passage would tell me "God sustains everything," but it doesn't. The verse tells me that Jesus sustains everything, and that He does so by the "mighty power of His command."

Obviously, and in a general way, Christ sustains us. Everyone is sustained by the universal common hand of Christ's mercy. He is the glue that makes natural laws hold together.

People go to surgery every day, and are further flung into danger often, and they often engage each circumstance prayer-less; and, without thought of God, they often get through fine. They could tell their stories about how the multitude of little things that should have gone wrong didn't; and that they were sustained just fine without any major effort devoted to prayer. They assume falsely, because they did not pray and include God, that they have been sustained, through difficulty, due to a coincidence, or thanks to natural laws.

Guess what? They are right in many ways. For it doesn't matter who we are, we still live in a world held together by the "mighty power of Christ's command." He commands the laws of this world to work. He is the space between atoms, and at the same time He is the bonding factor between the atoms. It doesn't matter if I think the laws of nature hold everything together, or if there is a God behind nature holding it all together. What we experience in this life is a world held together. If I believe there is a Designer, then I am likely to believe He is also the glue, the force, the energy behind the energy. Regardless, it works out the same for everyone; life is predictable because it is sustained by recurring laws.

Further, however, as a follower, I would be a fool to imagine there is not a specific hand of God on those who follow Jesus – those who pray, who ask, seek and knock. The Scriptures are too numerous on this subject to avoid.

(2 Chronicles 7:14; Proverbs 28:13; Isaiah 55:6; Ezekiel 18:27-30; Matthew 7:7; Matthew 21:22; Mark 11:24; Luke 11:9-13; James 1:5-6; 5:15; 1 John 3:22)

Here is a truth I have known for some time. My body, my life, was not all that conducive to surgery. It does not naturally fall under the general things held together by the mighty power of Christ's commands. When my cardiologist was giving me the percentages of all the things that could go wrong, he ended by saying, "Of course, these are not your chances, because you are not personally included in any of the studies." I could not be included in the studies because I had not had surgery yet.

There is no doubt in my mind I was one of those guys who, through surgery, would need something more than the general governing of the universe, by Christ. Natural laws were going to work in the reverse for me. I needed His specific touch, His specific care. No, I cannot know for certain what I am supposing here, but my spiritual instincts tell me I needed more than just the normal laws of statistics—I needed Christ.

There are things we encounter in life which, without Christ's specific intervention, would end up disastrous. All natural laws are held solid by "the mighty power of Christ's command" – car wrecks avoided, diseases battled and defeated in the immune system, should-have-beens thwarted, likelihoods reversed. However, also within the context of "the might power of Christ's command," is the infusion of insecurity, anxiety, strife, sin, hatred, malfunction, human error, genetic defect, and so on. All these things have their natural outworking and common endings. All these contrary activities are placed in the mix of what "Christ's mighty command holds together," and as much as we don't like it, the invasion of these other forces allows for disastrous potential.

Let me say it another way. There is so much wrong in the universe that Jesus holds together. There is the bonding together, for instance, of renegade forces that work against us, for our demise, on so many levels. Part of holding everything together is the allowing of adverse forces to work themselves out. It is in these times and circumstances we need the intervention of Christ.

Let me say this as clearly as I can. I knew, going into surgery, I needed more than the "mighty power of Christ's command" to get me through surgery. I was going to need specific intervention. It was my wife who lingered in the hours of God's intervention, not me. I was still under the anesthesia when she had to endure, and wait for God to do something outside of what I believe would've been the natural outcome. Let me be even clearer; apart from prayer, apart from all those who prayed (from churches in other nations to my own church and my own wife's intercession), all was necessary for me to come safely through and for Jesus to fulfill His promise to me, that "I will come to you." Prayer invited Jesus into an intervention in my life, so that the surgery, which for most would've been a slam dunk (but which for me had been difficult), was instead, for me, a Jesus intervention. Not everyone needs such an intervention in a surgery. I did.

CHAPTER 11

Whispers and Fog

I GET IT. NO MATTER WHO I AM, I GO THROUGH stuff. No matter who I am, the universal sustaining hand of God is upon me. No matter who I am, I live in a world being held together by Christ. And so I get it when the world whispers in my ear, "Why bother with prayer?"

In the fog of those whispers, I wander off into the misty woods of this world, a bit uncertain of where I am going, but I am complacently confident. I am complacently confident that in the end, the UFO of rapture will capture me and haul me off to heaven. After all, my ethics are pretty good. By pretty good, I mean just good enough to get me in. When the world wins in my head, and I succumb to the feeling of "why bother with prayer, I'm no pilgrim searching for a city coming down" I am merely seeking to ethically get by on this turf, long enough to get my ethical card punched.

I think the most insidious voice ringing in the ear of every follower of Jesus is this voice of pessimism – "why bother?" Pessimism questions leadership, motives, fairness, but – most of all – pessimism asks, "Why bother with prayer, why bother with the whole intervention thing?" Pessimism asserts that the world is quite nicely sustained without any extra effort on my part.

Maybe the voice of the world isn't "why bother?" maybe for others it is, "Why bother deeply or fervently, why not bother with prayer, but just superficially?"

My premise is simple. Jesus sustains the world by the power of His command, but He is wanting to do so much more. He is wanting more than anything to put the power of His command in the mouth of those who follow Him, not to sustain the world but to continue His work of transformation of the world; to continue to bring His new heaven and new earth into a reality.

As I have quoted, "The Son radiates God's own glory and expresses the very character of God, and he sustains everything by the mighty power of his command" (Hebrews 1:3 NLT).

The Greek word for "uphold" in Hebrews 1:3 has the thought to keep or maintain, but God wants to do so much more than merely keep or maintain our world. God is still making a new world out of the old one, and a new person out of the old one. His invitation is to study and discern; He is making all things new (Revelation 21:5). Jesus is out to create something new from this old world, and this new world will look the way Scripture describes it, where love, justice, mercy, grace and all other qualities described, will be the substance the earth is made of, and the condition in which the earth exists.

Who is a follower of Jesus? Those who think prayer is worth the bother. For in prayer, Scripture is declared, and the world begins to not be merely maintained, but reshaped in harmony with God's word. Prayer is a request for God to intervene, and God's promise is certain. When He is asked to intervene in harmony with His will, He does nothing less.

Isaac Watts's life would've been a life of insufferable misery, apart from his declarations, which we've come to know as hymns.

Jesus would've never fulfilled His ministry apart from His declaration of ministry purpose from Isaiah 61.

Many of the characters of Scripture whose lives were so flawed would've never amounted to anything apart from declarations, which is the key point of Hebrews 11.

There is no doubt that my surgery would've turned out differently without prayer declarations and the intervention of Jesus.

Yes, Jesus has defeated Satan, but He is further wanting to crush him, and that happens under our feet (Romans 16: 20).

CHAPTER 12

A Sober Note

Before I finish, I must take a moment to address a confusion. When my grandson Cruz was born, even before he was born, declarations were made over that child's life. When he was diagnosed, and the horror of disease descended upon our family, declarations were flying around the world. I have a file on my computer, tucked away, and in that file are my personal declarations and prayers for that little guy's life.

I knew from the beginning that he was in that part of creation where, despite the fact that Jesus holds the world together, outcomes can appear different than that which we'd most desire. So my prayer was in earnest. I was aware from the moment I knew he was to be a boy that he was in need of prayer and a special intervention from Jesus.

We cried, we prayed, we paced, we didn't sleep, we prayed some more; and in the end little Cruz died, and not even directly from the disease, but from the treatment. The pessimistic voice of the world could mock – "What good did all your bothering with prayer do?" Those voices were right, in a way – all of our arms miss holding him, especially his mother's, but I would argue against pessimism. Jesus did intervene; he did do and is doing miracles, even though He did not intervene as we had hoped.

I don't know how God finishes up His creation. I don't know how it will all look when the seventh trumpet will sound, and the kingdoms of this world will have become the the kingdom of our Lord (Revelation 11:15). But I do know that Cruz and all the other seeds planted in eternity will have a big part in what that world looks like. Not only Cruz, in fact. There are so many followers of Jesus on the earth today, so many who, with the word of the Lord on their lips, are planting the seeds of the new world God is creating for us.

I bring this story up, still tender to my soul, to say God does not promise to intervene to fulfill my will; God promises to intervene to fulfill His will. Some would say that if you only had faith, Cruz would not have died, and I would say the accuser on this point is absent of any comprehension of faith. There was no faith lacking. I have never seen such faith – not only in our family, but in each person close to us in prayer. It was the most amazing thing I have ever personally witnessed. If mere faith were the only prerequisite, Cruz would yet live. Here is the sobering truth – Jesus will intervene, Jesus will heal, Jesus will make a new world and a new person out of all who follow Him, but His intervention and His fulfilling of promises look much different to Him than to us. We have a timeline for God's promise, assuming it must be accomplished, the way we envision it, before we die, or else it might not be true. Jesus does not have an expiration date. Jesus was quite clear. He and the Father do not look at time and life the way we do. God has an ultimate destiny, and promises to fulfill it – a whole new world inhabited by the immortal lives of those He raises from the dead. Here on earth we are determining how we are sowing our lives, knowing that when we sow His word thoughout our life, we are sowing it into eternity (1 Corinthians 15: 42-44).

If you walked with us, through our time with Cruz, then you know God intervened many times. But you will also know part of his intervention was slipping Cruz immediately into His presence, for reasons known only to God. Yes, prayer causes Christ to intervene. Yes, most of His intervention happens this side of death. But the best part of His intervention will happen on the other side. And no, I will not ask God the proverbial 'why' questions. I will not ask why on a few occasions He didn't intervene this side of death, because when we see Him the answer will be so self-evident I won't need to ask. Cruz had purpose, Cruz has purpose. And when we see Jesus and Cruz, we will be well aware of what the purpose was.

The Romans passage holds true – yes, mostly before we die, but, if not, then through death He is working things together for the good.

"And we know that God causes everything to work together for the good of those who love God and are called according to his purpose for them" (Romans 8:29 NLT).

It is so important to make a mental note here. This verse is written in the context of prayer. Paul is simply saying he gets to a place where he is so overcome he doesn't know what to pray, what to declare. In that moment, a groan of pain in His heart, offered in the presence of Jesus, will turn the Holy Spirit loose to begin to pray. And the will of God prays through him. What is true for Paul is true for all, our groans in Jesus's presence release the Holy Spirit to pray and declare through us; and in the end God intervenes.

"And the Holy Spirit helps us in our weakness. For example, we don't know what God wants us to pray for. But the Holy Spirit prays for us with groanings that cannot be expressed in words. And the Father who knows all hearts knows what the Spirit is saying, for the Spirit pleads for us believers in harmony with God's own will" (Romans 8: 26-27 NLT).

We groaned all the way through our time with Cruz; the Holy Spirit, over and over again, would pray through us; and Jesus intervened; and we welcome, with joy, weeping and much hope, how God worked it to our good. Just because you don't get the outcome you want, don't give into the world's voice; don't be dominated by the words "Why bother?" As a follower, determine to pray and declare God's will over life. For there are many more interventions than we can ever imagine.

CHAPTER 13

Epilogue

I finally come to the chapter that I'd determined to write first, and that in fact had been the only thing I'd originally intended to write. Knowing the gracious hand of Jesus to intervene for me in this present trial has given me inspiration to share with you how I am led to pray more and more. Some might think, "He had surgery, God didn't heal him." From my vantage point, I look and say, "I had surgery, and I thrive apart from complications, or even death, because Christ has intervened."

The pessimist will ask me to prove it. You are right, I can't. But if you knew my internal heart and impressions over the past forty years, you'd know that Jesus intervened. As much as I appreciate the doctors and nurses, and the science on which they relied, I am one of those guys who needed Jesus to intervene. And He did, and I am so thankful.

A believer is happy to be sustained by God, but a follower further seeks for Jesus to intervene.

A believer is often happy with maintaining his trajectory in life, but a follower is one who is fervent to witness and to experience the miracle of transformation. A follower is not looking for Christ to maintain life, a follower is looking for Christ to transform life, and to create a world described in Scripture now, in seed form, before we experience the whole thing. A follower takes up the joyous effort of faith, declaring God's word true, while surrounded by the noisy voices of the world, which are vomiting all its discordant lies.

Here is how I form a declaration or prayer from Scripture.

Jesus Enters

Jesus enters my world afresh every day, as I head to my room for devotions. Jesus is at the center of my life, the first person I spend time with daily, the One I give my first day to weekly, the One I give the first of my income to always. Jesus has entered my life, He is God, not me. He has entered and I am changed.

How did Jesus enter my world? Romans 10:9-10 (NLT) says it best. "9 If you openly declare that Jesus is Lord and believe in your heart that God raised him from the dead, you will be saved. 10 For it is by believing in your heart that you are made right with God, and it is by openly declaring your faith that you are saved."

The heart believing, and the mouth confessing, that Jesus is Lord leads a soul to become well, saved, healthy. In verse 10, it becomes so clear – when a person believes in Jesus from the heart, trusting Him in all ways, that person is made right with God. No other action is necessary, just implicit trust makes a person right. Then, as a person begins to make declarations or confessions of what the heart believes, an amazing phenomenon occurs. the person experiences salvation, or wholeness.

If you want Jesus to fully enter your life, both actives are essential as a follower – complete trust, and open and shameless declaring. Jesus Enters, salvation or wholeness is experienced.

Joys Enters

Once Jesus entered my world, through faith and the confession of faith, I noticed something. I was full, really full of a joy from beyond myself. When faith and confession became a part of my existence, then Jesus's presence was experienced. And I must say He fills me with a joy unimaginable. Joy is an unimaginable provider of strength; it keeps you digging deeper in Christ, deeper into Scripture.

Scriptures Discovered

Because Jesus has entered, and because He comes with joy, I find myself drawn to Scripture. In the word I discover Jesus, and I discover how Jesus wants to intervene in my world. In the declaration I included in the first part of thisbook, the one I wrote before surgery, you will notice it was drawn from John 16. I had been meditating on that passage, while also thinking about Habakuk 2:4; Romans 1:17 and Galatians 3:11; and I sensed His voice within my mind highlighting certain phrases. I stopped, meditated, thought about what those words could mean in relationship to my upcoming surgery.

Scripture is not something I read to check a to-do list. I have people I pastor, those I pray for, family decisions I am making, financial needs, church decisions, leadership decisions – all of which need and require prayer and Scripture.

I am not good at general blessings or prayer; they bore me quickly. Bless my finances Lord, heal Billy-Bob, touch Myrtle, and you know what Frieda needs. I weary quickly of this kind of praying.

Scripture is where I go to find Christ's will. I read, meditate on it, discern God's will, and then write it down in the form of a "your kingdom come" type of prayer. I wanted to finish this booktoday, but I won't be able to, because I need to go visit someone in the hospital; and I need some time to read Scripture, discern God's will, and form a declaration to pray over this person. If God's holding of things together in a general way will not end well for this person, an intervention is needed.

Followers don't just pray general prayers, they don't use praying as a therapeutic balm for their hearts, they don't use prayer to get their own way. For the follower, prayer is an opportunity for Christ's will to intervene on earth, so that God's good can come together for those who love Him.

Declarations Formed

After having sensed God's will, I begin to write down what I see in the Scriptures I am meditating on. I write in a bold way. I write expecting Jesus to take over what I am writing to some degree, and to guide its content. I am always a bit amazed, because as I write the will of Christ as revealed in the Scripture, His will becomes more clear, and more focused.

In the declaration I included in the first chapter, you will notice it began with "I am not the ..." I don't know if I have ever begun a declaration with those words. When I did, I was uncomfortable, but I pressed on to see where it would lead. As I mentioned, when I finished I wondered if I should begin again. But I felt that the Lord gave me peace, so I left it alone.

Usually my declarations begin with, "Jesus you have" or "Jesus you have said". From there I just seek to let Him write through me, weaving in the Scripture, in order to declare God's will over the need I am focused upon. No, I do not think what

I write is perfectly from God, but it is fully from faith. It does capture to the best of my faith ability what I think Christ wants to do in a specific situation. I know there is more that I don't know than that which I do know, but I also know the declaration is faith-declared and Scripture-revealed; and so my sense is that God can do with it far more than I can visualize, even if it lacks in perfection.

If I am going to follow, if you are going to follow, we must do more than just believe in our hearts. We must confess.

Declarations Spoken

Finally, if we are going to overcome the voices of this world, we will need to declare these confessions in the face of our need. The truth about our needs cannot be what the world says it is; it must be what Jesus said, and what He is wanting us to do. When I declare something, it is God's last word on the subject. Not what comes later, not what works out in experience. God's word is the last word on the subject. No matter how everything looks, no matter how it seems it's going to turn out, I know this – the word of God abides forever, and what God says will be the ultimate outcome of the matter.

When Should We Declare?

If your business belongs to Jesus, then you will have a faith declaration, built from Scripture, over your business. So many people buy businesses, grow business, make business deals without a faith declaration guiding their business purposes. For followers, all business should begin in Scripture – God's will declared through one's mouth over one's vocation. Thus Jesus spoke to the rich young ruler – not to liquidate his business but to change its purpose and priority, so that his business would serve God, and His purposes (Acts 18:22-25).

If your finances belong to Jesus, then you will want a faith declaration over your finances. Your declaration should concern things like debt, and giving, and management, aligning it all with God's will.

If your family belongs to Jesus, then you will want a faith declaration over your family. You will see what Scripture has to say about health, transformation, discipline, destiny, and whatever else Christ leads you to include.

If your health belongs to Jesus, then you will want a faith declaration over your health, which might include what the Scripture says about eating, exercise, sleep and Sabbath.

If your spiritual and church life belong to Jesus, then you might want a faith declaration over what Scripture has to say about being planted in God's house, response to leadership, using your gifts, care for the hurting, worship, prayer, daily devotions.

Ultimately, you will encounter problems in your life. Friends or family will have needs, unexpected trials will come your way, and a faith declaration will be one of your best friends.

A faith confession, built from Scripture, without a doubt unleashes Jesus to intervene; and, as followers, this is one of our chief works. The word of God abides forever, and so declaring His will over any circumstance is like reshaping the world to God's eternal will.

I believe I am alive today because the "mighty voice of Christ" has sustained me. I also believe I am alive today because Jesus interrupted my life in response to a faith declaration.

Made in the USA
Coppell, TX
28 January 2023